OUTDOOR LIFE

essential

BOATING

for teens

Luke Thompson

Children's Press
A Division of Grolier Publishing
New York / London / Hong Kong / Sydney
Danbury, Connecticut

Book Design: Nelson Sa
Contributing Editor: Jennifer Ceaser
Photo Credits: Cover © Farrell Grehan/Corbis; p. 5 © Index Stock
Photography Inc.; p. 8 © Joel W. Rogers/Corbis; p. 11 © Patrick
Ward/Corbis; p. 13 © Neil Rabinowitz/Corbis; p. 14 © Kevin R.
Morris/Corbis; p. 17 © Paul A. Souders/Corbis; p. 18 © Index Stock
Photography Inc.; p. 21 © Joel W. Rogers/Corbis; p. 23 © Ken
Redding/Corbis; p. 24 © Index Stock Photography Inc.; pp. 26, 29 © Index
Stock Photography Inc,.; p. 32 © Kelly Mooney/Corbis; p. 34 © Neil
Rabinowitz/Corbis; p. 36© Joel W. Rogers/Corbis; p. 38 © Neil
Rabinowitz/Corbis; p. 41 © Neil Rabinowitz/Corbis.

Library of Congress Cataloging-in-Publication Data

Thompson, Luke.
  Essential boating for teens / by Luke Thompson.
    p. cm. – (Outdoor life)
  Includes bibliographical references and index.
  Summary: Presents the basics of boating, explaining the parts of the boat,
different types of boats, and safety tips.
  ISBN 0-516-23352-1 (lib. bdg.) – ISBN 0-516-23552-4 (pbk.)
  1. Boats and boating—Juvenile literature. [1. Boats and boating.] I. Title. II.
Outdoor life (Children's Press)

  GV775.3.T56 2000
  616.85'83—dc21

                                                              00-023360

CONTENTS

Introduction

Did you know that the Earth's surface is 70 percent water? That means there is more than twice as much water as there is land on our planet. There are oceans, rivers, lakes, and ponds. One way to appreciate all these bodies of water is from a boat.

Not only is boating a fun sport, it also is a great way to experience nature. There are many kinds of boats, and each offers different possibilities. You can spend the day on a lake, fishing from a rowboat. Maybe you'd rather spend the day with your family on a motorboat, taking turns waterskiing. Or perhaps you'd like to help man the decks of a sailboat on the high seas.

You may make a new friend while boating!

One way to experience the beauty of nature is to explore it by boat.

From the simplest rowboat to the most complicated yacht, all boating requires that you know the basics of water safety. You also should know the parts of a boat and how to navigate (steer) it. Some types of boating, such as sailing, may require a lot of training and practice. Other kinds of boating, such as canoeing, are easier to learn. You also need to think about which type of boating is available in the area where you live. For example, you won't be able to go deep-sea fishing regularly if you don't live near the ocean!

No matter which kind of boating you choose to do, it will be an exciting way to experience the open waters.

1
Boating Basics

A boat will float on the water's surface because of its
natural buoyancy.

It's important to know the basics of boating before you begin. As any sport does, boating has its own special set of terms.

HOW DO BOATS FLOAT?

When a boat is on the water, two forces act against it at the same time. The first is the force of gravity, which pulls down the boat. The second is a force called buoyancy, which is a boat's natural ability to float on water. As long as the force of buoyancy is greater than the force of gravity, a boat will stay on the surface.

Stability is what keeps a boat balanced and prevents it from capsizing (turning over). A boat may have all the buoyancy in the world, but it won't do much good if it's not balanced. When there is more weight on one side of the boat than on the other, it causes the boat to tip to one side. This is called heeling. Heeling too far to one side will cause a boat to capsize.

THE LANGUAGE OF BOATING

Boating terms may seem complicated at first, but they are a necessary part of the sport.

When people talk about the hull, they mean the main body of any boat. The hull does not include other equipment, such as a motor or sails. There are many terms that boaters use to describe the hull of their boat:

- The bow is the front end of the boat.
- The stern is the back end of the boat.
- Starboard is the right side of the boat (when looking forward).
- The port side is the left side of the boat (when looking forward).
- The beam is the width from port to starboard, at the boat's widest point.
- The keel is the center of the boat, running from bow to stern.

A boat needs to be secured to a dock by boat lines when it is not in use.

- Forward, or fore, is toward the front of the boat.
- Aft is toward the back of the boat.
- The amidships is the middle part of the boat.

Boat ropes (used to secure a boat to a dock) are called lines. Usually, there are at least three lines: the bow line, the stern line, and the spring line. The bow line secures the front, the stern line secures the back, and the spring line is at the boat's side.

CHOOSE YOUR BOAT

Boats are divided into two general types: powerboats and sailboats. Each type is based on how a boat is propelled (moved) through the water. Rowboats are considered powerboats because they are propelled using manpower. Some powerboats are motor-powered, such as speedboats. Sailboats include any type of boat powered by the wind. Even when a motor is used to move a sailboat, it is still considered a sailboat because of its sails.

A boat will float on any body of water, but some boats are designed for specific areas. Saltwater (ocean) crafts, such as coastal fishing boats, are built to hold up in rough seas. There also are saltwater flats boats, called this because of their flat-bottomed hulls. Flats boats allow anglers (people who fish) to go after the saltwater fish that live in shallow waters.

Freshwater crafts include rowboats, canoes, and bass boats. They are made to be used in

Sailboats are powered by the force of the wind.

freshwater areas, such as rivers and lakes, but not in rough seas. Freshwater boats usually are made with lighter materials, such as aluminum. For this reason, don't take these boats out on the ocean, where waves could capsize them.

2
Man-Powered Boats

One of the easiest man-powered boats to operate is
the simple rowboat.

Man-powered boats are the oldest form of boat. Man-powered boats include rowboats, canoes, and kayaks.

ROW, ROW, ROW YOUR BOAT

The rowboat is the most basic kind of boat. Rowboats come in all shapes and sizes, from a small rubber dinghy to a sleek, eight-person racing craft. Most rowboats are from 8 to 18 feet (2 to 5 m) in length and have a hull made of aluminum. All rowboats have oars, which extend out from the boat on either side. The simplest rowboat has two oars.

An oar has a handle, which hangs inside the boat. At the other end of an oar is a wide, flat blade, which sits in the water. An oar is fastened to the side of the boat by an oarlock.

It is much easier to pull the oars through the water than it is to push them. For this reason, most rowing is done facing aft. To row a boat, a person pulls the handles of the oars so that the blades swipe through the water. This is called a stroke. Your leg and back muscles should do most of the work when rowing.

Once you've taken a stroke, lift the oar blades out of the water and push the handles away from your body. This movement is called the recovery. A good recovery is one in which the blades of the oars don't touch the water. At the end of the recovery your arms should be fully extended again. Then let the blades drop back into the water and take another stroke.

Rowboats can be used for recreation, such as for fishing. Some types of rowboats, such as racing sculls, are used in competition. The sport of rowing boats is known as crew. The crew team usually is made up of eight people and a coxswain who tells the crew when to pull the oars.

Most canoes are light enough to carry.

CAN YOU CANOE?

Canoes are made of aluminum, fiberglass, plastic, lightweight wood, or rubber. They range from 11 to 20 feet (3 to 6 m) in length. Longer canoes are designed to hold more people. Canoes usually are only 2 to 3 feet (less than 1 m) wide, which is extremely narrow compared to other kinds of boats. Most canoes are light, weighing anywhere from 50 to 100 pounds (22.5 to 45 kg).

The most common canoe shape has a rounded bottom and a bow and stern that slope upward. Because of a canoe's narrow shape and light weight, it can easily capsize. Some canoes are made more stable by having flat bottoms, but even these are "tippy." To avoid tipping over in a canoe, you will want to keep all the weight in the center of the boat.

A canoeist powers the boat through the water by using a single paddle made of wood, aluminum, or plastic. A canoe paddle looks a lot like an oar. On one end there is a handle and, on the opposite end, a broad, flat blade.

Canoe paddles come in many different sizes. The bigger the paddle, the more strength you need to pull it through the water. People canoeing for the first time usually use aluminum paddles with short, narrow blades.

Paddling and steering a canoe is harder than it looks. There are two main strokes to learn. The first stroke is the bow stroke. To take a bow stroke, put one hand (the hand that is closest to the inside of the boat) on the top of the paddle. Then put the other hand several inches lower. Put the paddle in the water far in front of you. Then pull straight back along the side of the canoe. You will have to switch sides after every few strokes to avoid going in circles.

Canoes are narrow boats with an open hull and a bow and stern that slope upward.

The second kind of stroke is the j-stroke. The j-stroke is the most effective stroke because it combines the power of the bow stroke with steering. The j-stroke starts the same way as the bow stroke. Then, when the paddle is parallel to your hip, turn the blade sideways using your upper hand. Next, bring the paddle to the side of the boat and push out. This stroke, which is in the shape of a J, helps to keep the canoe straight.

When two people are canoeing, the person steering always sits in the back. The two canoeists also should be making strokes at the same time. If you get a chance to see a canoe race, you'll notice that the racers are always rowing exactly together.

CRAZY FOR KAYAKS

A kayak is, in some ways, like a canoe. A kayak is long and narrow with a rounded bottom. A paddle is used to power the boat through the

A kayak is similar to a canoe, but it has a closed hull and is usually built for just one person.

water. However, there are some ways in which a kayak differs from a canoe. Most kayaks are built to hold just one person, but canoes can hold several. Another difference is that a kayak usually has a closed deck, but a canoe has an open hull.

The kayaker sits in a cockpit with his legs inside the hull of the boat. The cockpit is the hole in the deck of the kayak. Then a spray skirt is placed around the kayaker's waist. A spray skirt is a sheet of waterproof material that prevents water from getting inside the shell of the kayak. Spray skirts are made out of light, synthetic (man-made) materials. The spray skirt allows kayakers to roll over without the kayak filling with water.

Kayakers also use different paddles than do canoeists. A kayak paddle has blades on both ends. When kayakers are moving in a straight line, they alternate their strokes from one side of the boat to the other. A canoeist does this too, but the kayaker doesn't have to lift the paddle across his or her body each time. In a sense, the kayaker has two canoe paddles joined together.

White-water kayaking is the most popular version of the sport. Kayaks can move very fast in rapids and are easy to maneuver.

White-water kayaking is an exciting way to experience the sport.

KEEP FROM CAPSIZING
About 90 percent of canoe and kayak capsizing occurs when people are getting onboard. Here's how to avoid tipping over:
- Place the boat in the water lengthwise, so that it is parallel to the shore. Wade ankle deep into the water.
- For canoes, squat down next to the boat and hold onto both sides of the boat. Shift your body so that most of your weight is over the center of the canoe. Then, step into the bottom center of the canoe and quickly kneel down.
- If there is more than one canoeist, one person should board the boat as above, while the other person holds the canoe steady.
- For kayaks, sit on the stern deck of the boat. Then slide into the cockpit, keeping your legs straight.
- Canoeists and kayakers should then use a paddle to push off from the shore into the water.

Most capsizing accidents with canoes occur before the boat is even out on the water.

3
Powerboats

Some powerboats are quite large and expensive,
such as this yacht.

Powerboats, which are powered by motors, are the most popular boats in North America. This is not exactly a surprise. For one thing, a motor never gets tired. Also, a motorboat doesn't require a windy day. And unlike a sailboat, it's easy to learn how to navigate a powerboat.

Powerboats range from 12-foot (3.5-m), thousand-dollar skiffs to 125-foot (38-m), multimillion-dollar yachts. A yacht is a powerboat measuring at least 30 feet (9 m) in length. Regardless of the size of the powerboat, they all have one thing in common: motors.

THE ENGINE THAT COULD

Powerboats come with one of two different kinds of engines (motors). The outboard engine hangs off the back of the boat and can be taken on and off. The inboard engine is built into the boat's hull. Outboard engines are good for smaller speedboats, and inboard motors usually are built into larger boats. Inboard engines are the more powerful engines and can move even the biggest yacht.

Both engine types work in the same way: by making the propeller turn. The propeller is a small, fanlike part of the motor. By turning beneath the water very quickly, the propeller pushes the boat across the water. Some recreational powerboats can go up to 100 miles (161 km) per hour. Boats designed for racing can go even faster.

GET YOUR MOTOR RUNNING

Many boat engines work in the same way as engines do in a car. They need gas to work. There is a key to turn the motor on and off. As a car engine does, a boat engine has gears: neutral (in which the boat doesn't move),

There are many features on a powerboat that are similar to those on a car—such as a steering wheel.

forward, and reverse. These gears are on the throttle, which looks like a lever with a handle. The throttle controls the boat's engine to give it more or less speed.

Starting a boat engine is a lot more complicated than starting a car. Here are the steps to start up your boat's motor:

- Turn the key to the "on" position. Check the fuel gauge to see that there is gas in the tank.
- Make sure that the gear is in the neutral position. On most motors, this means that the lever (throttle) will be pointed straight up.
- On some boat engines, you will have a choke. A choke is used during cold weather to give the engine extra fuel during start-up. Press in the choke for five to ten seconds. Then release the choke once the engine has warmed up.
- With the gear in neutral, push the throttle forward about an inch. Now start the

motor. The engine should start running in about ten seconds. Don't push it all the way forward or you will be giving the engine all its power.

- Let the engine run for about twenty seconds, then bring the throttle back to the idle position. The motor should be running. If the engine dies, restart it by following the same steps.

OFF YOU GO!

Before you move away from the dock, make sure that everyone is wearing a life jacket and that each person's hands are inside the boat. Then untie each of the lines that hold the boat to the dock. Now put the boat in gear, grab the steering wheel, and you're off!

Once you are out on the water, you can increase your speed by pushing the throttle forward. To slow down, bring your throttle back toward the neutral position. To brake, bring your boat to a speed of less than 10 miles

(16 km) per hour. Then put the gear into reverse to stop the boat.

If the boat begins bouncing up and down (like a bucking horse), you will want to increase your speed. However, don't try to make a sharp turn at a high speed or you could tip over.

Knowing Navigation

No matter what kind of boat you are on, you should learn some basic navigation skills. Navigation means plotting the course that a boat will follow. It involves knowing how to read a marine chart (a map of the water), a compass, and distances. A navigation class will teach you these skills, as well as educate you about underwater conditions that you may not be able to see.

Once you are out on the water, you can increase your speed by pushing the throttle forward.

4
Sailboats

Sailboats are more complicated to navigate than are other types of boats.

Sailboats are one of the most important vehicles in the history of the world. Sailboats ruled the globe for thousands of years until the motor was invented.

Sailboats are much more complicated than any other type of boat. Not only do sailboats have a lot more parts, they also are more difficult to navigate. It is necessary that you take a class to learn how to operate a sailboat. You never should try to learn how to sail on your own. The following information just skims the surface of what you need to know to be a sailor.

PARTS OF A SAILBOAT

The four parts of every sailboat are the hull, the sail, the spars, and the rigging. The hull is the main body of the boat. The sail is the piece of fabric through which the wind propels the

boat. The spars are the poles that hold up the sail. The rigging is all the ropes and lines used to support the spars and sails.

Spars

The largest of the spars' poles is the mast. The mast fits into the deck of the sailboat and stands straight up in the air. There are three different mast types: the foremast, the mainmast, and the mizzenmast. The foremast sits closest to the bow. The mainmast

On a sailboat, the foremast is at the front, the mainmast is at the center, and the mizzenmast is at the back.

comes out of the center of the boat. The mizzenmast sits to the stern of the mainmast.

The other poles are the booms and gaffs. The booms and gaffs are poles that run perpendicular to the mast. They hold the sail out to the side. The mast holds the sail up in the air. The difference between a boom and a gaff is that a boom goes on the bottom of the sail and a gaff goes on the top.

Sails

Just as there are different masts, there are different kinds of sails. There is a mainsail, a jib, a mizzensail, and a spinnaker. Some sailboats have more than one mast and sail. The number of masts and sails on a boat determines what kind of sailboat it is.

TYPES OF SAILBOATS

There are five common types of sailboats. A catboat has one mast and one sail. A sloop has one mast and two sails. A ketch has two masts and three sails. A yawl, as a ketch does, has two masts and three sails, but they are arranged differently. A schooner has two masts and more than three sails.

Some sailboats also have more than one hull. Catamarans have two hulls, and trimarans have three hulls.

HOIST THE SAIL!

Here are the most basic steps in preparing to sail:

- Lay the mainsail on the dock next to the boat.
- Hitch both the top and bottom of the mainsail to the pole.
- Point the boat into the wind so that the sail won't fill with air as you raise it.
- Hoist (raise) the sail up the pole by pulling on the rope.
- Adjust the tension of the sail using the ropes along the edge.

HOW TO CONTROL A SAILBOAT

To control a sailboat, you must know how to operate all these different parts. The main way to control a sailboat is by its rudder. The rudder is a flat piece of wood or fiberglass attached to the back of the boat. By turning the rudder, a sailor can change the direction of the hull as it moves across the water.

These boats each have a spinnaker, which is a large, triangle-shaped sail.

The rudder, however, is of little use by itself. It is just as important to have control over the sail as it is to have control over the hull. Without the lines to control it, a sail will just flap in the wind instead of catching the wind, as it should.

There are three basic maneuvers that a sailor must learn:

- **Sailing with the wind** To sail with the wind, a sail is put all the way out and the wind simply pushes the boat along in its direction.
- **Sailing against the wind** It is impossible to sail straight into the wind because the sail won't be able to use any of the wind's force. To sail against the wind requires tacking. To tack, a sailboat zigzags back and forth into the wind.
- **Sailing across the wind** This is the fastest way to sail. The wind is coming from the side of the boat. To catch the wind, the sail must be drawn in all the way. Sailing

across the wind sometimes lifts one side of the boat out of the water. This is called planing. Planing is extremely fun and gives sailors the sensation of great speed.

ENJOY BOATING

No matter where you live, there are sure to be places to go boating. Even if you don't know anyone who has a boat, you can always rent one for a day. Boat rentals, especially canoe rentals, are available in most areas. Decide which kind of boating you'd like to learn and study the boat's parts and how to navigate. Remember, learning the aspects of boating takes time, but it will be a very rewarding experience.

The fastest way to sail is across the wind, as this boat is doing.

Safety Tips

- There must be at least one life jacket for every person onboard the boat.
- Everyone must wear his or her life jacket while the boat is in the water.
- Wear shoes that have good tread.
- Protect yourself from the sun with a hat or visor, sunglasses, and sunscreen.
- If you're canoeing or kayaking in rough water, always wear a helmet.
- Before you go boating, make sure you tell an adult where you plan to go and when you will be back. This is called a float plan.
- Check the weather forecast before you go boating. Never attempt to take your boat out if there's the danger of a storm.
- Never lose sight of a person in the water. Turn off your boat's power immediately. If you're on a sailboat, turn the boat into the wind to stop it from moving forward. Toss a life preserver to the person.
- If you spring a leak, quickly fill the hole with a boat cushion, a piece of clothing, or an extra life jacket. You also can patch it with duct tape.
- If your boat capsizes, first take a head count and make sure everyone is safe. If you know you can

swim to shore easily, then go ahead. If there is any doubt, stay with the boat.

- Don't overload your boat before you head out into the water. Check the capacity that your boat can hold (there should be a sticker with this information on the hull).
- Keep alert to other boats on the water.
- Learn about the right-of-way and follow those rules. Sailboats and man-powered boats usually have right-of-way over powerboats.
- Don't ride on the bow or far side of the boat. If the boat stops or turns suddenly, you could fall overboard.

On your boat, you should have the following:

- whistle: to contact other boaters
- flashlight: to signal other boaters
- mirror: to signal during the daytime
- first aid kit: to patch up minor injuries
- pair of oars: to get the boat to shore if the motor dies
- blanket: to keep warm if someone gets wet
- fire extinguisher: in case there is a fire onboard

New Words

amidships the middle part of the boat

beam width from port to starboard, at the boat's widest point

booms and gaffs the parts of the spars that go perpendicular to the mast and hold the sail out to its full width

bow the front of a craft

bow line the rope that secures the front to a dock

bow stroke a straight stroke made in a canoe

buoyancy the force that keeps a boat floating on the water

capsize to tip over

centerboard a board on a sailboat that sticks down through the center of the hull

choke used during cold weather to give the engine extra fuel during start-up

cockpit a hole in the deck of the hull

foremast the mast that is closer to the bow than the mainmast

forward also called "fore," toward the front of the boat

heeling when a boat becomes unbalanced and shifts to one side

hull the main body of the boat

inboard engine a motor built into the hull of a larger boat

j-stroke a stroke used by a person steering a canoe that helps to turn the boat

keel the center line of any boat

mast the main spar of a sailboat; it rises vertically and holds up the sail

mizzenmast a mast that is further toward the stern than the mainmast

neutral a gear in which the boat doesn't move

oar a paddle with a wide, flat blade on one end and a handle on the other

oarlock a pivot that holds the oar on the side of a boat

outboard engine a motor used on smaller craft that can be taken on and off

planing when a sailboat moves across the wind and one side lifts out of the water

port the left side of the boat

propeller a fanlike part of the engine that physically moves the motorboat

recovery lifting the oar after a stroke so that the blade doesn't touch the water

rudder a board that hangs off the back of a sailboat and is used to steer

spars the poles used to keep a sail stretched to its fullest

spray skirt a lining of waterproof material stretched over the cockpit of a kayak

spring line the rope that secures the side of the boat to the dock

starboard the right side of the boat

stern the back of the craft

stern line the rope that secures the back of the boat to the dock

tacking a way to sail into the wind by zigzagging across the wind

throttle a lever that controls the boat's engine to give it more or less speed

Resources

Adventures at Sea

http://tqjunior.thinkquest.org/6169/home.html

Attend an online sailor's school, learn sailing terms, find out how to tie sailing knots, and read maps. Discover the history of sailing around the world.

American Canoe Association

7432 Alban Station Boulevard, Suite B-232

Springfield, VA 22150

Web site: *www.aca-paddler.org*

Learn everything you need to know about canoeing and kayaking, including how to paddle, how to carry your boat, and what equipment and clothing you'll need on your trip.

BoatSafe.com

www.boatsafe.com

Learn about boating courses, take a boating class online, get boating tips and safety tips. Also find out about navigation tools.

For Further Reading

Books

Armstrong, Bob. *Getting Started in Powerboating*. Camden, ME: International Marine Publishing, 1995.

Isler, Peter. *Let's Go Sailing*. New York: William Morrow & Co., 1993.

Sargeant, Frank. *The Complete Idiot's Guide to Boating and Sailing*. New York: Macmillian General Reference, 1998.

Siminoff, Roger. *Boating 101*. New York: McGraw-Hill, 1999.

Wing, Charles. *One Minute Guide to the Nautical Rules of the Road*. Camden, ME: International Marine Publishing, 1998.

Magazine

Boating World
2100 Powers Ferry Road
Atlanta, GA 30339
Web site: *www.boatingworldonline.com*

Index

About the Author

Luke Thompson was born in Delaware. He holds a degree in English literature from James Madison University. He lives in Vail, Colorado.